The Dolphin

ROBERT LOWELL

THE DOLPHIN

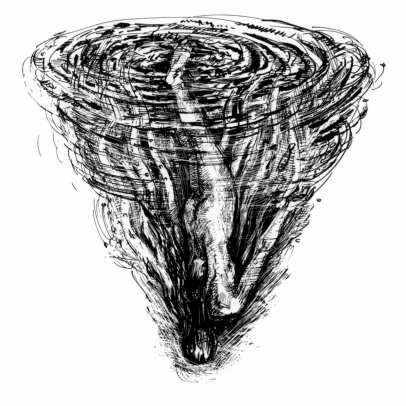

FARRAR, STRAUS AND GIROUX

NEW YORK

For Caroline

Contents

The Dolphin

Fishnet

Any clear thing that blinds us with surprise,
your wandering silences and bright trouvailles,
dolphin let loose to catch the flashing fish. . . .
saying too little, then too much.
Poets die adolescents, their beat embalms them,
the archetypal voices sing offkey;
the old actor cannot read his friends,
and nevertheless he reads himself aloud,
genius hums the auditorium dead.
The line must terminate.
Yet my heart rises, I know I've gladdened a lifetime
knotting, undoing a fishnet of tarred rope;
the net will hang on the wall when the fish are eaten,
nailed like illegible bronze on the futureless future

Redcliffe Square

1. Living in London

I learn to live without ice and like the Queen;
we didn't like her buildings when they stood,
but soon Victoria's manly oak was quartered,
knickknacks dropped like spiders from the whatnot,
grandparents and their unmarried staffs decamped
for our own bobbed couples of the swimming twenties,
too giddy to destroy the homes they fled.
These houses, no two the same, tremble up six stories
to dissimilar Flemish pie-slice peaks,
shaped by constructor's pipes and scaffolding—
aboriginal like a jungle gym.
Last century's quantity brick has a sour redness
that time, I fear, does nothing to appease,
condemned by age, rebuilt by desolation.

2. Window

Tops of the midnight trees move helter skelter
to ruin, if passion can hurt the classical
in the limited window of the easel painter—
love escapes our hands. We open the curtains:
a square of white-faced houses swerving, foaming,
the swagger of the world and chalk of London.
At each turn the houses wall the path of meeting,
and yet we meet, stand taking in the storm.
Even in provincial capitals,
storms will rarely enter a human house,
the crude and homeless wet is windowed out.
We stand and hear the pummelling unpurged,
almost uneducated by the world—
the tops of the moving trees move helter skelter.

3. *America from Oxford, May 1970*

The cattle have stopped on Godstow Meadow,
the peacock wheels his tail to move the heat,
then pivots changing to a wicker chair,
tiara of thistle on his shitty bobtail.
The feathertouch of May in England, but the heat
is American summer. Two weeks use up two months;
at home the colleges are closed for summer,
the students march, Brassman lances Cambodia—
he has lost his pen, his sword folds in his hand like felt.
Is truth here with us, if I sleep well?—
the ten or twelve years my coeval gives himself
for the new bubble of his divorce . . . ten or twelve years—
this air so estranged and hot I might be home. . . .
We have climbed above the wind to breathe.

4. *Oxford*

We frittered on the long meadow of the Thames,
our shoes laminated with yellow flower—
nothing but the soft of the marsh, the moan of cows,
the rooster-peacock. Before we had arrived,
rising stars illuminated Oxford—
the Aztecs knew these stars would fail to rise
if forbidden the putrifaction of our flesh,
the victims' viscera laid out like tiles
on fishponds changed to yellow flowers,
the goldfinchnest, the phosphorous of the ocean
blowing ambergris and ambergris,
dolphin kissing dolphin with a smirking smile,
not loving one object and thinking of another.
Our senses want to please us, if we please them.

5. *The Serpent*

In my dream, my belly was yellow, panels
of mellowing ivory, splendid and still young,
though slightly ragged from defending me.
My tan and green backscales were cool to touch.
For one who has always loved snakes, it is no loss
to change nature. My fall was elsewhere—
how often I made the woman bathe in her waters.
With daylight, I'd turn small, a small snake
on the river path, arrowing up the jags.
Like this, like this, as the great clock clangs round,
I see me—a green hunter who leaps from turn to turn,
a new brass bugle slung on his invisible baldric;
he is groping for trout in the private river,
wherever it opens, wherever it happens to open.

6. *Symptoms*

A dog seems to lap water from the pipes,
a wheeze of dogsmell and dogcompanionship—
life-enhancing water brims my bath—
(the bag of waters or the lake of the grave. . . .?)
from the palms of my feet to my wet neck—
I have no mother to lift me in her arms.
I feel my old infection, it comes once yearly:
lowered good humor, then an ominous
rise of irritable enthusiasm. . . .
Three dolphins bear our little toilet-stand,
the grin of the eyes rebukes the scowl of the lips,
they are crazy with the thirst. I soak,
examining and then examining
what I really have against myself.

7. *Diagnosis: to Caroline in Scotland*

The frowning morning glares by afternoon;
the gay world in purple and orange drag,
Child-Bible pictures, perishables:
oranges and red cabbage sold in carts.
The sun that lights their hearts lights mine?
I see it burn on my right hand, and see
my skin, when bent, is finely wrinkled batwing.
Since you went, our stainless steelware ages,
like the young doctor writing my prescription:
The hospital. My twentieth in twenty years. . . .
Seatrout run past you in the Hebrides—
the gay are psychic, centuries from now,
not a day older, they'll flutter garish colors,
salmontrout amok in Redcliffe Square.

Hospital

1. Shoes

Too many go express to the house of rest,
buffooning, to-froing on the fringe of being,
one foot in life, and little right to that:
"I had to stop this business going on,
I couldn't attack my doctor anymore,
he lost his nerve for running out on life. . . ."
"Where I am not," we chime, "is where I am."
Dejection washes our pollution bare.
My shoes? Did they walk out on me last night,
and streak into the glitter of the blear?
I see two dirty white, punctured tennis-shoes,
empty and planted on the one-man path.
I have no doubt where they will go. They walk
the one life offered from the many chosen.

2. Juvenilia

Person, place and thing, once violated,
join the rubbish that predated nature;
boys race the hooded highway lights untimed,
and tiptoe through the treasuries of smashed glass,
scavenging for a lifelike hand or head.
I hoped to find girls in the wide, white squares;
I had no names or numbers—I could not meet them,
the women had suffered a fate worse than death—
weird in London of the bullhorn God.
No rocket goes as far astray as man. . . .
I'm on bounds, I mark my proofs, a sheaf of tapeworms,
sleek, untearable, interminable
paper that slices my finger like a knife—
one time in fifty, God will make a date.

3. *Rival*

Is there an ur-dream better than words, an almost
work of art I commonplace in retelling
through the fearfullness of memory,
my perfunctory, all-service rhythms? . . .
For long, our taxi is changing into a van—
you-I . . . beefing we've not seen our driver.
He moves through the tan canvas-lapped bales of the van,
his step is careless, the bales begin to converge.
I am happy because I recognize
the man who assaulted you yesterday. . . .
Much later, the man's face, tan, a Chinese portrait,
floats symmetrical in a pool the same color.
It takes seconds to see the rival is dead,
the same water washes in and out of the mouth.

4. *Stairwell*

Climbing from chair to chair to chair to chair,
I dare not look the stairwell in the eye;
its underpinning soils like carbon paper,
each step up would stop an athlete's heart—
the stairwell is hollow, bored, unbearable,
the same six words repeating on a disk:
marching for peace with paranoia marching,
marching for peace with paranoia marching . . .
ever at my heels and stormily.
Darling, we have halved the ailing summer.
Did the beheaded wish himself in half?
He was so airily cool and free and high—
or did he wish the opposite like us,
when we stitched two summer months in one?

5. Walter Raleigh

Horseguard and Lifeguard, one loud red, one yellow,
colorful and wasteful and old hat. . . .
Americans can buy them on a postcard—
we do not see them with hallucinated eyes,
these horsemen, smartly antiqued and resurrected
from the blood of Crimea and Waterloo,
free to ramble London or trample France. . . .
Here sitting at your feet I feel no pressure
of analogies binding us to them.
Our omen is Raleigh kneeling for the axe—
he isn't going to die, it's not been painted.
Our Raleigh is a small boy in his velvet
and courting dress hearing an old buffer
lie about the toothless Spanish Main.

6. Double-Vision

I tie a second necktie over the first;
no one is always waiting at the door,
and fills the window . . . sometimes a Burmese cat,
or maybe my Daughter on the shell of my glasses.
I turn and see persons, my pajama top
loose-knotted on the long thin neck of a chair—
make yourself at home. The cat walks out—
or does it? The room has filled with double-shadows,
sedation doubles everything I see. . . .
You can't be here, and yet we try to talk;
somebody else is farcing in your face,
we haggle at cross-purposes an hour.
While we are talking, I am asking you,
"Where is Caroline?" And you *are* Caroline.

Hospital II

1. Voices

"What a record year, even for us—
last March, I knew you'd manage by yourself,
you were the true you; now finally
your clowning makes visitors want to call a taxi,
you tease the patients as if they were your friends,
your real friends who want to save your image
from this genteel, disgraceful hospital.
Your trousers are worn to a mirror. . . . That new creature,
when I hear her name, I have to laugh.
You left two houses and two thousand books,
a workbarn by the ocean, and two slaves
to kneel and wait upon you hand and foot—
tell us why in the name of Jesus." Why
am I clinging here so foolishly alone?

2. Letter

"In London last month I encountered only
exhausted traffic and exhausting men—
the taxi driver might kill us, but at least he cared."
Cold summer London, your purer cold is Maine,
where each empty sweater and hollow bookcase hurts,
every pretext for their service gone.
We wanted to be buried together in Maine . . .
you didn't, "impractical, cold, out of touch."
The terrible postcards you bought and stamped for me
go off to Harriet, the Horseguards, the Lifeguards,
the Lord Mayor's Chariot, Queen Bess who could not bear—
true as anything else to fling a child. . . .
I shout into the air, my voice comes back—
nothing reaches your black silhouette.

3. *Old Snapshot from Venice 1952*

From the salt age, yes from the salt age,
courtesans, Christians fill the churchyard close;
that silly swelled tree is a spook with a twig for a head.
Carpaccio's Venice is as wide as the world,
Jerome and his lion lope to work unfeared. . . .
In Torcello, the stone lion I snapped behind you,
venti anni fa, still keeps his poodled hair—
wherever I move this snapshot, you have moved—
it's twenty years. The courtesans and lions
swim in Carpaccio's brewing tealeaf color.
Was he the first in the trade of painting to tell tales? . . .
You are making Boston in the sulfury a.m.,
dropping Harriet at camp, Old Love,
Eternity, You . . . a future told by tealeaves.

Caroline

1. *Flashback to Washington Square 1966*

Two babies in your stroller, perhaps three,
all four of you in Bloomingdale polo coats;
they seemed to rush on one course, you another—
your brute joy in slanting them to the curb. . . .
We were Sunday people gone before we met.
We meet too many people, wives and husbands;
the family lasts, the child is never weaned,
parents never err in guessing wrong. . . .
How mean the drink-money for the hour of joy,
its breathy charity and brag of body. . . .
I hesitate to argue for our love unloosed—
we earn less credit than we burn,
though joy in the moment crowns credulity,
dying to be what we are.

2. *Fragility*

One foot in last year, one in last July,
the motionless month, the day that lasts a month.
We reach mid-journey, you lag by fifteen summers,
half a year more than Harriet's whole life.
The clock looks over my shoulder crazily.
This hospital is tinder . . . retards the sun,
melancholia sprinkles the blind root,
the cat nibbles little shoots foretelling rain,
sultry August is my wandering eye.
Hope grows less malign or thinks it might,
I wait for the hospital to catch on fire.
Keep me in your shadow . . . gold grizzling your undyed hair,
frail body of an athlete, her big hand—
your honor is humor and fragility.

3. *July-August*

In hospital I read the news to sleep:
the Fourth of July, Bastille Day, the 16th
your Birthday . . . my two-month bankholiday.
August is summer lost in England.
Green nettles prick the oversoil with acid,
eat up the vestiges of last summer's clearing. . . .
One simultaneous sickness was enough
for us. From Brighton to Folkestone, the heads lie prone,
the patients mend, the doctors die in peace,
plucking the transient artificial flower—
the father fails to mail a single lobster
or salty nude to prove his pilgrimage.
I have no one to stamp my letters . . . I love you,
a shattered lens to burn the clinging smoke.

4. *Marriage?*

"I think of you every minute of the day,
I love you every minute of the day;
you gone is *hollow, bored, unbearable.*
I feel under some emotional anaesthetic,
unable to plan or think or write or feel;
mais ca ira, these things will go, I feel
in an odd way against appearances,
things will come out right with us, perhaps.
As you say, we got across the Godstow Marsh,
reached Cumberland and its hairbreadth Roman roads,
climbed Hadrian's Wall, and scared the stinking Pict.
Marriage? That's another story. We saw
the diamond glare of morning on the tar.
For a minute had the road as if we owned it."

5. *Morning Blue*

The bathwater honks in and in, ten minutes, twenty,
twists of fire and cooling jobless bubbles;
I am exposed, keep guessing if I can take
the chill of the morning and its dressing.
The bathroom is a daub of daylight,
the beefy, flustered pigeons swish their quills—
in time the pigeons will forget the window;
I cannot—I, in flight without a ledge.
Up the carpetted stairway, your shoes clack,
clack nearer, and absentmindedly withdraw,
life withdrawn like a bad lead in poker.
Life *is* withdrawn, but after all it will be. . . .
It's safer outside; in the open air,
the car flying forward to hit us, has room to swerve.

Summer Between Terms

1.

The day's so calm and muggy I sweat tears,
the summer's cloudcap and the summer's heat. . . .
Surely good writers write all possible wrong—
are we so conscience-dark and cataract-blind,
we only blame in others what they blame in us?
(The sentence writes *we*, when charity wants *I*. . . .)
It takes such painful mellowing to use error. . . .
I have stood too long on a chair or ladder,
branch-lightning forking through my thought and veins—
I cannot hang my heavy picture straight.
I can't see myself . . . in the cattery,
the tomcats doze till the litters are eatable,
then find their kittens and chew off their breakable heads.
They told us by harshness to win the stars.

2.

Plains, trains, lorries simmer through the garden,
the reviewer sent by God to humble me
ransacking my bags of dust for silver spoons—
he and I go on typing to go on living.
There are ways to live on words in England—
reading for trainfare, my host ruined on wine,
my ear gone bad from clinging to the ropes.
I'd take a lower place, eat my toad hourly;
even big frauds wince at fraudulence,
and squirm from small incisions in the self—
they live on timetable with no time to tell.
I'm sorry, I run with the hares now, not the hounds.
I waste hours writing in and writing out a line,
as if listening to conscience were telling the truth.

Fall Weekend at Milgate

1.

The day says nothing, and lacks for nothing . . . God;
but it's moonshine trying to gold-cap my life,
asking fees from the things I lived and loved,
pilgrim on this hard-edge Roman road.
Your portrait is fair-faced with your honesty,
the painter, your first husband, made girls stare.
Your wall mirror, a mat of plateglass sapphire,
mirror scrolls and claspleaves, shows this face,
huge eyes and dawn-gaze, rumination unruffled,
unlearning apparently, since 1952. . . .
I watch a feverish huddle of shivering cows;
you sit making a fishspine from a chestnut leaf.
We are at our crossroads, we are astigmatic
and stop uncomfortable, we are humanly low.

2.

The soaking leaves, green yellow, hold like rubber,
longer than our eyes glued to the window can take;
none tumble in the inundating air . . . .
A weak eye sees miracles of birth in fall,
I'm counterclockwise . . . did we fall
last April in London, late fifties in New York?
Autumn sops on our windshield with huge green leaves;
the seasons race engines in America
burying old lumber without truce—
leaf-blight and street dye and the discard girl . . .
the lover sops gin all day to solve his puzzle.
Nature, like philosophers, has one plot,
only good for repeating what it does well:
life emerges from wood and life from life.

3.

Milgate kept standing for four centuries,
good landlord alternating with derelict.
Most fell between. We're landlords for the weekend,
and watch October go balmy. Midday heat
draws poison from the Jacobean brick,
and invites the wilderness to our doorstep:
moles, nettles, last Sunday news, last summer's toys,
bread, cheeses, jars of honey, a felled elm
stacked like construction in the kitchen garden.
The warm day brings out wasps to share our luck,
suckers for sweets, pilots of evolution;
dozens drop in the beercans, clamber, buzz,
debating like us whether to stay and drown,
or, by losing legs and wings, take flight.

Records

". . . I was playing records on Sunday,
arranging all my records, and I came
on some of your voice, and started to suggest
that Harriet listen: then immediately
we both shook our heads. It was like hearing
the voice of the beloved who had died.
All this is a new feeling . . . I got the letter
this morning, the letter you wrote me Saturday.
I thought my heart would break a thousand times,
but I would rather have read it a thousand times
than the detached unreal ones you wrote before—
you doomed to know what I have known with you,
lying with someone fighting unreality—
love vanquished by his mysterious carelessness."

In Harriet's Yearbook

You must be strong through solitude, said Fate,
for the present this thought alone must be your shelter—
this in your yearbook by your photograph.
Your bearing is a woman's not full woman,
bent to a straw of grass just plucked and held
like an eyetest card—you mature in blacking out.
A girl can't go on laughing all the time.
The other campgirls sway to your brooding posture,
they too must scowl to see a blade of grass;
yet you are out of focus and blurred like me,
separation stoops and fogs the lens—
one more humiliation to blow away,
only husked out in monosyllable—
profundities too shallow to expose.

Communication

"These communications across the sea,
but for once you were almost buoyant—
phone-conversations get so screwed . . . I wish
I had your lovely letter in my hand
delivered to me by the stately Alex
just the minute you hung up. I'm off
to Dalton to pick up Harriet's grades and record—
it is frightening to be a soul,
marked in the Book of Judgment once a month,
because you haven't lived much, and are alive.
Things go on, Pained Heart, another month is gone. . . .
She stayed up talking to us all last night,
giving three brainy women back their blast.
Age is nice . . . if that's your age . . . thirteen."

Dream

For months the heat of love has kept me marching,
now I am healthy, and I cannot stand;
women see through me like a head of cheese.
Boys on a gold enamelled goiterband:
boys in ultra-violet tights and doublets,
from the costume shop of Botticelli,
albino Absaloms; they probe my thicket
with pikes and wingnets, and I try to breathe,
I try to keep up breathing when I hide.
This is not Florence, or German mercenaries;
this is England, main artery of fighting—mercy was murder
at Towton when King Edward's heralds counted
twenty thousand Lancastrian dead in the field,
doubling the number killed to make the count.

Mermaid

I have learned what I wanted from the mermaid
and her singeing conjunction of tail and grace.
Deficiency served her. What else could she do?
Failure keeps snapping up transcendence,
bubble and bullfrog boating on the surface,
belly lustily lagging three inches lowered—
the insatiable fiction of desire.
None swims with her and breathes the air.
A mermaid flattens soles and picks a trout,
knife and fork in chainsong at the spine,
weeps white rum undetectable from tears.
She kills more bottles than the ocean sinks,
and serves her winded lovers' bones in brine,
nibbled at recess in the marathon.

2.

Baudelaire feared women, and wrote, "Last night, I slept
with a hideous negress." Woe to Black Power,
woe to French women and the Academicians.
Why do I blush the moon with what I say?
Alice-in-Wonderland straight gold hair,
fair-featured, curve and bone from crown to socks,
bulge eyes bigger than your man's closed fist,
slick with humiliation when dismissed—
you are packaged to the grave with me,
where nothing's opened by the addressee . . .
almost a year and almost my third wife,
by accepting, by inviting, by surmounting,
rushing the music when the juice goes dead—
float like a butterfly and sting like a bee.

3.

Our meetings are no longer like a screening;
I see the nose on my face is just a nose,
your *bel occhi grandi* are just eyes
in the photo of you arranged as figurehead
or mermaid on the prow of a Roman dory,
bright as the morning star or a blond starlet.
Our twin black and tin Ronson butane lighters
knock on the sheet, are what they are,
too many, and burned too many cigarettes. . . .
Night darkens without your necessary call,
it's time to turn your pictures to the wall;
your moon-eyes water and your nervous throat
gruffs my directive, "*You must go now go.*"
Contralto mermaid, and stone-deaf at will. •

4.

I see you as a baby killer whale,
free to walk the seven seas for game,
warm-hearted with an undercoat of ice,
a nerve-wrung back . . . all muscle, youth, intention,
and skill expended on a lunge or puncture—
hoisted now from conquests and salt sea
to flipper-flapper in a public tank,
big deal for the Sunday ennui. . . . My blind love—
on the Via Veneto, a girl
counting windows in a glass café,
now frowning at her menu, now counting out
neanderthals flashed like shorebait on the walk. . . .
Your stamina as *inside-right* at school
spilled the topheavy boys, and keeps you pure.

5.

One wondered who would see and date you next,
and grapple for the danger of your hand.
Will money drown you? Poverty, though now
in fashion, debases women as much as wealth.
You use no scent, dab brow and lash with shoeblack,
willing to face the world without more face.
I've searched the rough black ocean for you,
and saw the turbulence drop dead for you,
always lovely, even for those who had you,
Rough Slitherer in your grotto of haphazard.
I lack manhood to finish the fishing trip.
Glad to escape beguilement and the storm,
I thank the ocean that hides the fearful mermaid—
like God, I almost doubt if you exist.

The Mermaid Children

In my dream, we drove to Folkestone with the children,
miles of ashflakes safe for their small feet;
most coasts are sand, but this had larger prospects,
the sea drained by the out-tide to dust and dunes
blowing to Norway like brown paper bags.
Goodbye, my Ocean, you were never my white wine.
Only parents with children could go to the beach;
we had ours, and it was brutal lugging,
stopping, teasing them to walk for themselves.
When they rode our shoulders, we sank to our knees;
later we felt no weight and left no footprints. . . .
Where did we leave them behind us so small and black,
their transisters, mermaid fins and tails,
our distant children charcoaled on the sky?

They

Why are women a fraction more than us?
Lie with a woman and wake with Liberation,
her bondage is our lash, her labor our dismissal.
Her witness bugles to my dubious shade:
Woman victorious, animosity dead.
(Will the worm turn and sting her victor heel?)
Stendhal knew women deserved an education:
"No civilization rests on its best men,
its highest level, the mothers of its children—"
no vacation from shepherding the lost children . . .
if a mother no longer cares for her children,
civilization sinks to its institutions,
says, "Your fucking little psychopaths,
I didn't ask for them, they came for me."

The Friend

Your long arms antlered on the Goth-rude fireplace,
a frame ample and worthy of your wingspread . . .
whatever we say is for our hearts alone—
the first confidence of our two souls at school,
now seasoned with retrospective mercy.
Some meaning never has a use for words,
truth one couldn't tell oneself on the toilet,
self-knowledge swimming to the hook, then turning—
in Latin we learned no subject is an object.
"You say you'll remarry, you can't take none or two. . . .
All this makes me think of one thing, *you,*
at your age . . . think of it, it's the one big item
on your agenda—Do you really want
to live in the same room with anyone?"

In the Mail

"Your student wrote me, if he took a plane
past Harvard, at any angle, at any height,
he'd see a person missing, *Mr. Robert Lowell.*
You insist on treating Harriet as if she
were thirty or a wrestler—she is only thirteen.
She is normal and good because she had normal and good
parents. She is threatened of necessity. . . .
I love you, Darling, there's a black black void,
as black as night without you. I long to see
your face and hear your voice, and take your hand—
I'm watching a scruffy, seal-colored woodchuck graze
on weeds, then lift his greedy snout and listen;
then back to speedy feeding. He weighs a ton,
and has your familiar human aspect munching."

Doubt

1. *Draw*

The cardtable is black, the cards are played face down,
black-backs on a black cloth; and soon by luck
I draw a card I wished to leave unchosen,
and discard the one card I had sworn to hold.
Dreams lose their color faster than cut flowers,
but I remember the number on my card,
a figure no philosopher takes to bed. . . .
Should revelation be sealed like private letters,
till all the beneficiaries are dead,
and our proper names become improper Lives?
Focus about me and a blur inside;
on walks, things nearest to me go slow motion,
obscene streetlife rushes on the wheelrim,
steel shavings from the vacillating will.

2. *Pointing the Horns of the Dilemma*

From the dismay of my old world to the blank
new—water-torture of vacillation!
The true snakepit isn't monodrama Medea,
the gorgon arousing the serpents in her hair;
it's a room to walk with no one else, to walk,
take thought, unthink the thought and listen for nothing:
"She loves me too much to have my welfare at heart . . .
*they just aren't up to your coming home
three weeks, then leaving for a year. They just aren't.
They can't stand much more of anything,
they are so tired and hurt and worn. They go on,
knowing your real sickness is a fretful
deafness to little children . . . and suspect
it's impossible for anyone to help you.*"

3. *Critic*

Is my doubt, last flicker of the fading thing,
an honorable subject for conversation?
Do you know how you have changed from the true you?
I would change my trueself if I could:
I am doubtful . . . uncertain my big steps.
I fear I leave many holes for a quick knife
to take the blown rose from its wooden thorns.
A critic should save her sharpest tongue for praise.
Only blood-donors retain the gift for words;
blood gives being to everything that lives,
even to exile where tried spirits sigh,
doing nothing the day because they think
imagination matures from doing nothing,
hoping for choice, the child of vacillation.

Winter and London

1. *Closed Sky*

A hundred mornings greet the same closed sky,
one of nature's shows, one mantle wrapping
the dust of London with the dust of Europe—
in the interiors it is always night.
The clouds are welcome to us as insulation,
a silencer to the ultimate blue sky,
naked heaven's monologue with man.
In my country, the wettest Englishman
sparkles with approbation, magnifying
curious small things I could never see—
under closed sky, trifles are luminous,
gossip makes New York and London one,
one mouth . . . we use identical instruments
for putting up a house and pulling down.

2. *At* Offado's

The Latin Quarter abuts on Belgravia,
three floors low as one, blocks built of blocks,
insular eighteenth century laying down
the functional with a razor in its hand,
construction too practical for conservation.
An alien should count his change here, bring a friend.
Usually on weekend nights I eat alone;
you've taken the train for *Milgate* with the children.
At *Offado's*, the staff is half the guests,
the guitar and singers wait on table,
the artist sings things unconsolable:
"Girls of Majorca. Where is my Sombrero?
Leave me alone and let me talk and love me—
a cod in garlic, a carafe of cruel rosé."

3. *Flounder*

In a day we pass from the northern lights
to doomsday dawns. Crowds crush to work at eight,
and walk with less cohesion than the mist;
the sky, without malice, is acid, Christmas lights
are needed to reveal the Thames. God sees—
wash me as white as the sole I ate last night,
acre of whiteness, back of Folkestone sand,
cooked and skinned and white—the heart appeased.
Soles live in depth, see not, spend not . . . eat;
their souls are camouflaged to die in dishes,
flat on their backs, the posture of forgiveness—
squinch-eyes, bubbles of bloodshot worldliness,
unable ever to turn the other cheek—
at sea, they bite like fleas whatever we toss.

4. *Mastodon*

They splashed red on the Jews about to be killed,
then ploughed them back and forth in captured tanks;
the wood was stacked, the chainsaw went on buzzing.
In the best of worlds, the jailors follow the jailed.
In some final bog, the mastodon,
curled tusks raised like trumpets to the sky,
sunk to their hips and armpits in red mud,
splashed red for irreversible liquidation—
the heavens were very short of hearing then.
The price of freedom is displacing facts:
gnashed tusk, bulk-bruised bulk and a red splash.
Good narrative is cutting down description;
nature sacrifices heightening
for the inevitable closing line.

5. Freud

Is it honorable for a Jew to die as a Jew?
Even the German officials encouraged Freud
to go to Paris where at least he was known;
but what does it matter to have a following,
if no one, not even the concierge, says *good day*?
He took a house in London's amused humdrum
to prove that Moses must have been Egyptian—
"What is more monstrous than outliving your body?"
What do we care for the great man of culture—
Freud's relations were liquidated at Belsen,
Moses Cohn who had nothing to offer culture
was liquidated at Belsen. Must we die,
living in places we have learned to live in,
completing the only work we're trained to do?

6. Harriet's Donkey

On this blank page no worse, not yet defiled
by my inspiration running black in type,
I see your sepia donkey laugh at me,
Harriet's doodle, me in effigy,
my passport photo to America
that enflames the soul and irritates the eye—
M. de Maupassant va s'animaliser.
Gloomier exiles brought their causes here,
and children crying up and down the stairs;
Freud found his statue, older Jewish prophets
bit in until their teeth had turned to chalk,
found names in London and their last persona,
a body cast up lifeless on this shore. . . .
Family, my family, why are we so far?

During a Transatlantic Call

We can't swing New York on Harry Truman incomes—
the bright lights dragging like a ball and chain,
the Liberal ruined by the Liberal school.
This was the price of your manic flight to London—
the closed provincial metropolis, never
an asylum for the mercurial American mind. . . .
They say fear of death is a child's remembrance
of the first desertion. My daughter knows no love
that doesn't bind her with presents, letters, visits,
things outward and visible. . . . I've closed my mind
so long, I want to keep it closed, perhaps—
I have no faith in my right to will transcendence,
when a house goes, the species is extinct. . . .
They tell me to stop, they mustn't lose my money.

Exorcism

1.

What we love we are. As November
hardens the morning hoarfrost, I grow small;
slowly the bridal fury shows white teeth,
parading in invisible link mail—
greenness slurs into sterility,
the landscape is New England textile gray.
You point your finger: *What you love you are.*
I know what it is for a woman to be left,
to wait in the ante-room of apprehension:
Inasmuch as I am loved I am—
a woman romanticizing her exorcist,
two souls in a cocoon of mystery.
Your woman dances for you, child in arms,
she is dancing for you, Baby-Skull-Smile.

2.

This morning, as if I were home in Boston, snow,
the pure witchery-bitchery of kindergarten winters;
my window whitens like a movie screen,
glaring, specked, excluding rival outlook—
I can throw what I want on this blank screen,
but only the show already chosen shows:
Melodrama with her stiletto heel
dancing bullet wounds in the parquet.
My words are English, but the plot is hexed:
one man, two women, the common novel plot . . .
what you love you are. . . .
You can't carry your talent with you like a suitcase.
Don't you dare mail us the love your life denies;
do you really know *what you have done?*

Plotted

Planes arc like arrows through the highest sky,
ducks *V* the ducklings across a puckered pond;
Providence turns animals to things.
I roam from bookstore to bookstore browsing books,
I too maneuvered on a guiding string
as I execute my written plot.
I feel how Hamlet, stuck with the Revenge Play
his father wrote him, went scatological
under this clotted London sky.
Catlike on a paper parapet,
he declaimed the words his prompter fed him,
knowing convention called him forth to murder,
loss of free will and licence of the stage.
Death's not an event in life, it's not lived through.

The Couple

"Twice in the past two weeks I think I met
Lizzie in the recurrent dream.
We were out walking. *What sort of street*, you ask,
fair or London? It was our own street.
What did you hear and say? We heard ourselves.
The sidewalk was two feet wide. We, arm in arm,
walked, squelching the five-point oakleaves under heel—
happily, they melted under heel.
Our manner had some intimacy in my dream.
What were you doing on this honeymoon?
Our conversation had a simple plot,
a story of a woman and a man
versifying her tragedy—
we were talking like sisters . . . you did not exist."

Before Woman

1. *Before the Dawn of Woman*

"Gazing close-up at your underjaw,
a blazon of barbaric decoration,
a sprinkle of black rubies, clots from shaving,
panting in measure to your wearied breath,
I see the world before the dawn of woman,
a jungle of long-horned males, their scab of rapine,
rhinoceros on Eden's rhinoceros rock. . . .
You hold me in the hollow of your hand—
a man is free to play or free to slack,
shifty past the reach of ridicule.
A woman loving is serious and disarmed,
she is less distracted than a pastured mare,
munching as if life depended on munching. . . .
Like the animals, I am humorless."

2. *Day*

Even a green parrot can talk one book,
sing up his second-rate, most writers do;
Christians and women have thought all men are evil,
though nothing living wholly disappoints God.
Living with you is living a long book
War and Peace, from day to day to day,
unable to look off or answer my name.
My springless step still stalks for youngman's wildweed,
the goldfinch-nest defying euphemism,
the God-borne instant never letting up.
Where will you take me in the fizz of winter?
Darling, the cork, though fat and black, still pulls,
new wine floods our prehistoric veins—
the day breaks, impossible, in our bed.

Artist's Model

1.

Hölderlin's thing with swan-scene and autumn
behind was something beautiful, wasn't it?
Manet's bottles mirrored behind his bar-girl
are brighter than the stuff she used to serve—
the canvas should support the artist's model.
Our children and theirs will have to pose for themselves;
we squeezed the juice, their job to eat the skin,
we put God on his knees, and now he's praying. . . .
When I sit in my bath, I wonder why
I haven't melted like a cube of sugar—
fiction should serve us with a slice of life;
but you and I actually lived what I have written,
the drunk-luck venture of our lives sufficed
to keep our profession solvent, was peanuts to live.

2.

"My cousin really learned to loathe babies,
she loved to lick the palate of her Peke,
as if her tongue were trying a liqueur—
what I say should go into your *Notebook*. . . .
I'd rather dose children on morphine than the churches.
When you are dying, and your faith is sick,
and you go on flapping in your sheets
like a cockroach fallen in a fishbowl;
you will look for the love you fumbled, and see
only religion caught naked in the searchlights—
Christians scream worse than atheists on the death-ward.
What is so infamous about it is
they shove your bed nearer the door to move the corpse;
you know damn well it isn't for fresh air."

3.

"*If it were done, 'twere well it were done quickly*—
to quote a bromide, your vacillation
is acne." And we totter off the strewn stage,
knowing tomorrow's migraine will remind us
how drink heightened the brutal flow of elocution. . . .
We follow our plot obediently as actors,
divorced from making a choice by our need to act.
"If you woke and found an egg in your shoe,
would you feel you'd lost this argument?"
It's over, my clothes fly into your borrowed suitcase,
the good day is gone, the broken champagne glass
crashes in the ashcan . . . private whims, and illusions,
too messy for our character to survive.
I come on walking off-stage backwards.

4.

Our dream has been more than life is solid—
I touch your house, the price of the furniture,
the two round marble tables big as millwheels
in your parlor unvulgarized by clutter-comforts.
But I can say more than this about you,
equal your big eyes to a silver tablespoon,
hindsight cannot romance their anger away—
bite of dog or dolphin, laughing and meant.
In my dream of misinterpretation,
your midnight taxi meets the midnight train—
one person removed, the household falls askew
from the children's tea to toilet paper.
I read in the floorboards' unintelligible worm-script
the blanks for all our birthdays . . . yours by summer.

Mermaid Emerging

The institutions of society
seldom look at a particular—
Degas's snubnosed dancer swings on high,
legging the toplights, never leaving stage,
enchanting lovers of art, discerning none.
Law fit for all fits no one like a glove. . . .
Mermaid, why are you another species?
"Because, you, I, everyone is unique."
Does anyone ever make you do anything?
"Do this, do that, do nothing; you're not chained.
I am a woman or I am a dolphin,
the only animal man really loves,
I spout the smarting waters of joy in your face—
rough weather fish, who cuts your nets and chains."

Marriage

1. *Angling*

Withdrawn to a third your size, and frowning doubts,
you stare in silence through the afterdinner,
when wine takes our liberty and loosens tongues—
fair-face, ball-eyes, profile of a child,
except your eyelashes are always blacked,
each hair colored and quickened like tying a fly.
If a word amuses you, the room includes your voice,
you are audible; none can catch you out,
your flights are covered by a laughing croak—
a flowered dress lost in the flowered wall.
I am waiting like an angler with practice and courage;
the time to cast is now, and the mouth open,
the huge smile, head and shoulders of the dolphin—
I am swallowed up alive . . . I am.

2. *Tired Iron*

Mulch of tired iron, bullet-stitch of straffing planes—
surely the great war of our youth was hollow;
still it had cleanness, now the smelly iron,
the war on reeds, the grand *noyades* of the rice-fields.
We promised to put back Liberty on her feet . . .
I can't go on with this, the measure is gone:
a waterfall, the water white on green,
like the white letters on my olive keyboard—
to stray with you and have you with me straying,
flesh of my body, saved by our severalness—
you will not marry, though disloyal to woman
in your airy seizures of submission,
preferring to have your body broken to being
unbreakable in this breaking life.

3. *Gruff*

The sky should be clearing, but it cannot lighten,
the unstable muck flies through the garden trees,
there's morning in my heart but not in things.
We've almost made a marriage like our parents—
the poise of disaster! Our love means giving the wheel
a shake that scatters spurs of displaced bone
in the heel of the driver's hand; it means to turn
right angle on ourselves, on our external star.
We might have married as Christ says man must not
in heaven where marriage is not, and giving
in marriage has the curse of God and Blake.
I am in bondage here, and cannot fly;
when marriage is surmounted, what is left?
"Heaven, if such things are," you gruff into the phone.

4. *Leaf-Lace Dress*

Leaf-lace, a simple intricate design—
if you were not inside it, nothing much,
bits of glinting silver on crinkled lace—
you fall perhaps metallic and as good.
Hard to work out the fact that makes you good,
whole spirit wrought from toys and nondescript,
though nothing less than the best woman in the world.
Cold the green shadows, iron the seldom sun,
harvest has worn her swelling shirt to dirt.
Agony says we cannot live in one house,
or under a common name. This was the sentence—
I have lost everything. I feel a strength,
I have walked five miles, and still desire to throw
my feet off, be asleep with you . . . asleep and young.

5. *Knowing*

This night and the last, I cannot play or sleep,
thinking of Grandfather in his last poor days.
Caroline, he had such naked nights,
and brought his *tortures of the damned* to breakfast—
when his son died, he made his grandchildren plant trees;
his blood lives, not his name. . . . We have our child,
our bastard, easily fathered, hard to name . . .
illegibly bracketed with us. My hand
sleeps in the bosom of your sleeping hands,
firm in the power of your impartial heat.
I'm not mad and hold to you with reason,
you carry our burden to the narrow strait,
this sleepless night that will not move, yet moves
unless by sleeping we think back yesterday.

6. *Gold Lull*

This isn't the final calm . . . as easily,
as naturally, the belly of the breeding
mother lifts to every breath in sleep—
I feel tomorrow like I feel today
in this gold lull of sleep . . . the muzzled lover
lies open, takes on the world for what it is,
a minute more than a minute . . . as many a writer
suffers illusions that his phrase might live:
power makes nothing final, words are deeds.
President Lincoln almost found this faith;
once a good ear perhaps could hear the heart
murmur in the square thick hide of Lenin
embalmed, wide-eyed in the lull that gives a mother
courage to be merciful to her child.

7. *Green Sore*

We wake too early, the sun's already up,
the too early chain-twitter of the swallows fatigues,
words of a moment's menace stay for life:
not that I wish you entirely well, far from it.
That was my green life, even heard through tears. . . .
We pack, leave *Milgate*, in a rush as usual
for the London train, leaving five lights burning—
to fool the burglar? Never the same five lights.
Sun never sets without our losing something,
keys, money—not everything. "Dear Caroline,
I have told Harriet that you are having a baby
by her father. She knows she will seldom see him;
the physical presence or absence is the thing."—
a letter left in a page of a book and lost.

8. *Letter*

"I despair of letters. You say I wrote H. isn't
interested in the thing happening to you now.
So what? A fantastic untruth, misprint, something;
I meant the London scene's no big concern, just you. . . .
She's absolutely beautiful, gay, etc.
I've a horror of turmoiling her before she flies
to Mexico, alone, brave, half Spanish-speaking.
Children her age don't sit about talking *the thing*
about their parents. I do talk about you,
and I have never denied I miss you . . .
I guess we'll make Washington this weekend;
it's a demonstration, like all demonstrations,
repetitious, gratuitous, unfresh . . . just needed.
I hope nothing is mis-said in this letter."

9. *Heavy Breathing*

Your heavier breathing moves a lighter heart,
the sun glows on past midnight on the meadow,
willing, even in England, to stretch the day.
I stand on my head, the landscape keeps its place,
though heaven has changed. Conscience incurable
convinces me I am not writing my life;
life never assures which part of ourself is life.
Ours was never a book, though sparks of it
spotted the page with superficial burns:
the fiction I colored with first-hand evidence,
letters and talk I marketed as fiction—
but what is true or false tomorrow when surgeons
let out the pus, and crowd the circus to see us
disembowelled for our afterlife?

10. *Late Summer at* Milgate

A sweetish smell of shavings, wax and oil
blows through the redone bedroom newly aged;
the sun in heaven enflames a sanded floor.
Age is our reconciliation with dullness,
my varnish complaining, *I will never die.*
I still remember more things than I forgo:
once it was the equivalent of everlasting
to stay loyal to my other person loved—
in the fallen apple lurked a breath of spirits,
the uninhabitable granite shone
in Maine, each rock our common gravestone. . . .
I sit with my staring wife, children . . . the dour Kent sky
a smudge of mushroom. In temperate years the grass
stays green through New Year—I, my wife, our children.

11. *Ninth Month*

For weeks, now months, the year in burden goes,
a happiness so slow burning, it is lasting;
our animated nettles are black slash
by August. Today I leaned through lunch on my elbows,
watching my nose bleed red lacquer on the grass;
I see, smell and taste blood in everything—
I almost imagine your experience mine.
This year by miracle, you've jumped from 38
to 40, joined your elders who can judge:
woman has never forgiven man her blood.
Sometimes the indictment dies in your forgetting.
You move on crutches into your ninth month,
you break things now almost globular—
love in your fullness of flesh and heart and humor.

12. *Before Hospital*

I ask doggishly into your face—
dogs live on guesswork, heavens of submission,
but only the future answers all our lies—
has perfect vision. A generation back,
Harriet was this burdensome questionmark—
we had nowhere then to step back and judge the picture. . . .
I fish up my old words, *Dear* and *Dear Ones*;
the dealer repeats his waterfall of cards—
will the lucky number I threw down
come twice? Living is not a numbers game,
a poor game for a father when I am one. . . .
I eat, drink, sleep and put on clothes up here,
I'll get my books back when we've lived together—
in this room on which all other rocks bear down.

13. *Robert Sheridan Lowell*

Your midnight ambulances, the first knife-saw
of the child, feet-first, a string of tobacco tied
to your throat that won't go down, your window heaped
with brown paper bags leaking peaches and avocados,
your meals tasting like Kleenex . . . too much blood is seeping . . .
after twelve hours of labor to come out right,
in less than thirty seconds swimming the blood-flood:
Little Gingersnap Man, homoform,
flat and sore and alcoholic red,
only like us in owning to middle-age.
"If you touch him, he'll burn your fingers."
"It's his health, not fever. Why are the other babies so pallid?
His navy-blue eyes tip with his head. . . . Darling,
we have escaped our death-struggle with our lives."

14. *Overhanging Cloud*

This morning the overhanging clouds are piecrust,
milelong Luxor Temples based on rich runny ooze;
my old life settles down into the archives.
It's strange having a child today, though common,
adding our further complication to
intense fragility.
Clouds go from dull to dazzle all the morning;
we have not grown as our child did in the womb,
met Satan like Milton going blind in London;
it's enough to wake without old fears,
and watch the needle-fire of the first light
bombarding off your eyelids harmlessly.
By ten the bedroom is sultry. You have double-breathed;
we are many, our bed smells of hay.

15. *Careless Night*

So country-alone, and O so very friendly,
our heaviness lifted from us by the night . . .
we dance out into its diamond suburbia,
and see the hill-crown's unrestricted lights—
all day these encroaching neighbors are out of sight.
Huge smudge sheep in burden becloud the grass,
they swell on moonlight and weigh two hundred pounds—
hulky as you in your white sheep-coat, as nervous to gallop. . . .
The Christ-Child's drifter shepherds have left this field,
gone the shepherd's breezy too predictable pipe.
Nothing's out of earshot in this daylong night;
nothing can be human without man.
What is worse than hearing the late-born child crying—
and each morning waking up glad we wake?

16. *Morning Away from You*

This morning in oystery Colchester, a single
skeleton black rose sways on my flour-sack window—
Hokusai's hairfine assertion of dearth.
It wrings a cry of absence. . . . My host's new date,
apparently naked, carrying all her clothes
sways through the dawn in my bedroom to the shower.
Goodmorning. My nose runs, I feel for my blood,
happy you save mine and hand it on,
now death becomes an ingredient of my being—
my Mother and Father dying young and sixty
with the nervous systems of a child of six. . . .
I lie thinking myself to night internalized;
when I open the window, the black rose-leaves
return to inconstant greenness. A good morning, as often.

Another Summer

1. *Wildrose*

A mongrel image for all summer, our scene at breakfast:
a bent iron fence of straggly wildrose glowing
below the sausage-rolls of new-mown hay—
Sheridan splashing in his blue balloon tire:
whatever he touches he's told not to touch
and whatever he reaches tips over on him.
Things have gone on and changed, the next oldest
daughter bleaching her hair three shades lighter with beer—
but if you're not a blonde, it doesn't work. . . .
Sleeping, the always finding you there with day,
the endless days revising our revisions—
everyone's wildrose? . . . And our golden summer
as much as such people can. When most happiest
how do I know I can keep any of us alive?

2. *Dolphins*

Those warmblooded watchers of children—*do not say*
I have never known how to talk to dolphins,
when I try to they just swim away.
We often share the new life, *the new life*—
I haven't stilled my New England shades by combing
the Chinese cowlicks from our twisted garden,
or sorted out the fluff in the boiler room,
or stumbled on the lost mouth of the cesspool.
Our time is shorter and brighter like the summer,
each day the chill thrill of the first day at school.
Coughs echo like swimmers shouting in a pool—
a mother, unlike most fathers, must be manly.
Will a second dachshund die of a misborn lung?
Will the burned child drop her second boiling kettle?

3. *Ivana*

Small-soul-pleasing, loved with condescension,
even through the cro-magnon tirades of six,
the last madness of child-gaiety
before the trouble of the world shall hit.
Being chased upstairs is still instant-heaven,
not yet tight-lipped weekends of voluntary scales,
accompanying on a recorder carols
rescored by the Sisters of the Sacred Heart in Kent.
Though burned, you are hopeful, experience cannot tell you
experience is what you do not want to experience.
Is the teenager the dominant of ache?
Or flirting seniles, their conversation three noises,
their life-expectancy shorter than the martyrs?
How all ages hate another age,

and lifelong wonder what was the perfect age!

4. *Alimony*
(A DREAM IN THE FUTURE)

3, 4, and then 5 children, fortunately
fortune's hostages and not all ours—
the sea comes in to us, we move it outward. . . .
I'm somewhere, nowhere; four Boston houses I grew from,
slash-brick expressionist New England fall;
I walk, run, gay with frost . . . with Harriet . . .
a barracuda settlement. (Santo Domingo,
quick divorces, solid alimony,
its dictator's marina unsafe because of sharks
checking in twice daily like grinning, fawning puppies
for our sewage, even for their own excrement. . . .)
"I am not sure I want to see her again."
Harriet laughing without malice . . . with delight:
"That's how mother talks about you."

5. *The New*   (*Caroline*)

The one moment that says, *I am, I am, I am.* . . .
My girlfriends tell me I must stay in New York,
one never has such new friends anywhere;
but they don't understand,
wherever he is is my friend.

Leaving America for England

1. *America*

My lifelong taste for reworking the same water—
a day is day there, America all landscape,
ocean monolithic past weathering;
the lakes are oceans, nature tends to gulp. . . .
Change I earth or sky I am the same;
aging retreats to habit, puzzles repeated
and remembered, games repeated and remembered,
the runner trimming on his mud-smooth path,
the gamefish fattening in its narrow channel,
deaf to the lure of personality.
May the entertainment of uncertainty
help me from seeing through anyone I love. . . .
Overtrained for England, I find America . . .
under unmoved heaven changing sky.

2. *Lost Fish*

My heavy step is treacherous in the shallows—
once squinting in the sugared eelgrass for game,
I saw the glass torpedo of a big fish,
power strayed from unilluminating depth,
roaming through the shallows worn to bone.
I was seven, and fished without a hook.
Luckily, Mother was still omnipotent—
a battered sky, a more denuded lake,
my heavy rapier trolling rod bent *L*,
drowned stumps, muskrat huts, my record fish,
its endless waddling outpull like a turtle. . . .
The line snapped, or my knots pulled—I am free
to reach the end of the marriage on my knees.
The mud we stirred sinks in the lap of plenty.

3. *Truth*

Downstairs the two children's repeating piano duet,
when truth says goodmorning, it means goodbye.
The scouring voice of 1930 Oxford,
"Nothing pushing the personal should be published,
not even Proust's *Research* or Shakespeare's *Sonnets*,
a banquet of raw ingredients in bad taste. . . .
No Irishman can understate or drink. . . .
W. B. Yeats was not a gent,
he didn't tell the truth: *and for an hour,*
I've walked and prayed—who prays exactly an hour?
Yeats had bad eyes, saw nothing . . . not even peahens:
What has a bard to do with the poultry yard?
Dying, he dished his stilts, wrote one good poem,
small penance for all that grandeur of imperfection."

4. *No Telling*
(FOR CAROLINE)

How much less pretentiously, more maliciously
we talk of a close friend to other friends
than shine stars for his festschrift! Which is truer—
the uncomfortable full dress of words for print,
or wordless conscious not even no one ever sees?
The best things I can tell you face to face
coarsen my love of you in solitary.
See that long lonesome road? It must end
at the will and second of the end-all—
I am still a young man not done running around. . . .
The great circuit of the stars lies on jewellers' velvet;
be close enough to tell me when I will die—
what will love do not knowing it will die?
No telling, no telling . . . not even a last choice.

5. *Sick*

I wake now to find myself this long alone,
the sun struggling to renounce ascendency—
two elephants are hauling at my head.
It might have been redemptive not to have lived—
in sickness, mind and body might make a marriage
if by depression I might find perspective—
a patient almost earns the beautiful,
a castle, two cars, old polished heirloom servants,
Alka Seltzer on his breakfast tray—
the fish for the table bunching in the fishpond.
None of us can or wants to tell the truth,
pay fees for the over-limit we caught, while floating
the lonely river to senility
to the open ending. Sometimes in sickness,

we are weak enough to enter heaven.

6. *Facing Oneself*

After a day indoors I sometimes see
my face in the shaving mirror looks as old,
frail and distinguished as my photographs—
as established. But it doesn't make one feel
the temptation to try to be a Christian.

Foxfur

"I met Ivan in a marvelous foxfur coat,
his luxurious squalor, and wished you one . . . your grizzled
knob rising from the grizzled foxfur collar.
I long to laugh with you, gossip, catch up . . . or down;
and you will be pleased with Harriet,
in the last six months she's stopped being a child,
she says God is just another great man,
an ape with grizzled sideburns in a cage.
Will you go with us to *The Messiah*,
on December 17th, a Thursday,
and eat at the *Russian Tearoom* afterward?
You're not under inspection, just missed. . . .
I wait for your letters, tremble when I get none,
more when I do. Nothing new to say."

On the End of the Phone

My sidestepping and obliquities, unable
to take the obvious truth on any subject—
why do I do what I do not want to say?
When everything matters, ask and never know?
Your rapier voice—I have had so much—
hundred words a minute, piercing and thrilling . . .
the invincible lifedrive of everything alive,
ringing down silver dollars with each word. . . .
Love wasn't what went wrong, we kept our daughter;
what a good father is is no man's boast—
to be still friends when we're no longer children. . . .
Why am I talking from the top of my mouth?
I am talking to you transatlantic,
we're almost talking in one another's arms.

Cars, Walking, etc., an Unmailed Letter

"In the last three days Sheridan learned to walk,
and left the quadruped behind—for some reason
small pets avoid him. . . ." Who shakes hands with a dead friend?
I see a huge, old rattling brown paper bag,
a picture, no fact; when I try to unwrap it,
it slips in my hands. It is our old car
resurrected from the must of negligence,
warning like Hector's Ghost from the underground—
the car graveyard . . .
I do not drive in England, yet in my thought,
our past years, especially the summers, are places
I could drive back to if I drove a car,
our old Burgundy Ford station-wagon summer-car,
our fourth, and first not prone to accident.

Flight to New York

1. Plane-Ticket

A virus and its hash of knobby aches—
more than ever flying seems too lofty,
the season unlucky for visiting New York,
for telephoning kisses transatlantic. . . .
The London damp comes in, its smell so fertile
trees grow in my room. I read Ford's *Saddest Story*,
his *triangle* I read as his student in Nashville.
Things that change us only change a fraction,
twenty-five years of marriage, a book of life—
a choice of endings? I have my round-trip ticket. . . .
After fifty so much joy has come,
I hardly want to hide my nakedness—
the shine and stiffness of a new suit, a feeling,
not wholly happy, of having been reborn.

2. With Caroline at the Air-Terminal

"London Chinese gray or oyster gray,
every appalling shade of pitch-pitch gray—
no need to cook up far-fetched imagery
to establish a climate for my mood. . . .
If I have had hysterical drunken seizures,
it's from loving you too much. It makes me wild,
I fear. . . . We've made the dining-room his bedroom—
I feel unsafe, uncertain you'll get back.
I know I am happier with you than before.
Safer . . ." The go-sign blazes and my plane's
great white umbilical ingress bangs in place.
The flight is certain. . . . Surely it's a strange joy
blaming ourselves and willing what we will.
Everything is real until it's published.

3. *Purgatory*

In his portrait, mostly known from frontispiece,
Dante's too identifiable—
behind him, more or less his height, though less,
a tower tapering to a fingerend,
a snakewalk of receding galleries:
Purgatory and a slice of Europe,
less like the fact, more like the builder's hope.
It leans and begs the architect for support,
insurance never offered this side of heaven.
The last fifty years stand up like that;
people crowd the galleries to flee
the second death, they cry out manfully,
for many are women and children, but the maker
can't lift his painted hand to stop the crash.

4. *Flight*

If I cannot love myself, can you?
I am better company depressed . . .
I bring myself here, almost my best friend,
a writer still free to work at home all week,
reading revisions to his gulping wife.
Born twenty years later, I might have been prepared
to alternate with cooking, and wash the baby—
I am a vacation-father . . . no plum—
flown in to New York. . . . I see the rising prospect,
the scaffold glitters, the concrete walls are white,
flying like Feininger's skyscraper yachts,
geometrical romance in the river mouth,
conical foolscap dancing in the sky . . .
the runway growing wintry and distinct.

5. New York Again

After London, the wind, the eye, my thoughts
race through New York with gaping coarse-comb teeth,
the simple-minded streets are one-way straight,
no queues for buses and every angle right,
a bunchy London with twenty times the soaring;
it is fish-shaped, it is modern, it is metal,
austerity assuaged with melodrama,
an irritable reaching after fact and reason,
a love of features fame puts up for sale—
love is all here, and the house desolate.
What shall I do with my stormy life blown towards evening?
No fervor helps without the favor of heaven,
no permissive law of nature picks up the bill—
survival is talking on the phone.

6. No Messiah

Sometime I must try to write the truth,
but almost everything has fallen awry
lost in passage when we said goodbye in Rome.
Even the licence of my mind rebels,
and can find no lodging for my two lives.
Some things like death are meant to have no outcome.
I come like someone naked in my raincoat,
but only a girl is naked in a raincoat.
Planesick on New York food, I feel the old
Subway reverberate through our apartment floor,
I stop in our Christmas-papered bedroom, hearing
my *Nolo*, the non-Messianic man—
drop, drop in silence, then a louder drop
echoed elsewhere by a louder drop.

7. *Death and the Maiden*

Did the girl in *Death and the Maiden* fear marriage?
No end to the adolescence we attained
by overworking, then struggled to release—
my bleak habit of counting off minutes on my fingers,
like pages of an unrequested manuscript—
that brilliant onetime moment we alone shared,
the leftovers from God's picnic and old times.
Why do I weep for joy when others weep?
One morning we saw something, half weed, half wildflower,
rise from the only thruhole in the barn floor—
it had this chance in a hundred to survive.
We knew that it was someone in disguise,
a silly good person . . . thin, pealnosed, intruding,
the green girl who doesn't know how to leave a room.

8. *New York*

A sharper air and sharper architecture—
the old fashioned fishingtackle-box skyscrapers,
flesh of glass and ribs of tin . . . derisively
called *modern* in 1950, and now called modern.
As if one had tried to make polar bears
live in Africa—some actually survived,
curious, strong meat permutations of polar bear. . . .
It wasn't so once, O it wasn't so,
when I came here ten or twenty years ago. . . .
Now I look on it all with a yellow eye;
but the language of New Yorkers, unlike English,
doesn't make me fear I am going deaf. . . .
Last night at four or five, whenever I woke up,
I found myself crying—not too heavily.

9. *Sleepless*

Home for the night on my ten years' workbed,
where I asked the facing brick for words, and woke
to my conscious smile of self-incrimination,
hearing then as now the distant, panting siren,
small as a harbor boat patrolling the Hudson,
persistent cry without diminishment
or crescendo through the sleepless hours.
I hear its bland monotony, the voice
that holds, and never shortcircuits the transcendence
I fiddled for imperiously and too long.
All my friends are writers. Do I deserve
to sleep, because I gave myself the breaks,
self-seeking with persistent tenderness
rivals seldom lavish on a brother?

10. *New York*

I can move around more . . . through the thirty years
to the New York of Jean Stafford, Pearl Harbor, the Church?
Most of my old friends are mostly dead,
entitled to grow infirm and lap the cream—
if time that hurt so much improved a little?
Our onslaught, not wholly Pyrrhic, to launch Harriet
on the heart-turning, now savage, megapolis. . . .
A friendly soft depression browns the air,
it's not my glasses needing a handkerchief . . .
it's as if I stood tiptoe on a chair
so that I couldn't help but touch the ceiling—
almost obscenely, complaisantly on the phone with
my three wives, as if three-dimensional space were my breath—
three writers, none New Yorkers, had their great years there.

76

11. *Christmas*

All too often now your voice is too bright;
I always hear you . . . commonsense, though tense . . .
waking me to myself: truth, the truth, until
things are just as if they had never been.
I can't tell the things we planned for you this Christmas.
I've written my family not to phone today,
we had to put away your photographs.
We had to. We have no choice—we, I, they? . . .
Our Christmas tree seems fallen out with nature,
shedding to a naked cone of triggered wiring.
This worst time is not unhappy, green sap
still floods the arid rind, the thorny needles
catch the drafts, as if alive—I too,
because I waver, am counted with the living.

12. *Christmas*

The tedium and déjà-vu of home
make me love it; bluer days will come
and acclimatize the Christmas gifts:
redwood bear, lemon-egg shampoo, home-movie-
projector, a fat book, sunrise-red, inscribed
to me by Lizzie, "Why don't you lose yourself
and write a play about the fall of Japan?"
Slight spirits of birds, light burdens, no grave duty
to seem universally sociable
and polite. . . . We are at home and warm,
as if we had escaped the gaping jaws—
underneath us like a submarine,
nuclear and protective like a mother,
swims the true shark, the shadow of departure.

Dolphin

My Dolphin, you only guide me by surprise,
a captive as Racine, the man of craft,
drawn through his maze of iron composition
by the incomparable wandering voice of Phèdre.
When I was troubled in mind, you made for my body
caught in its hangman's-knot of sinking lines,
the glassy bowing and scraping of my will. . . .
I have sat and listened to too many
words of the collaborating muse,
and plotted perhaps too freely with my life,
not avoiding injury to others,
not avoiding injury to myself—
to ask compassion . . . this book, half fiction,
an eelnet made by man for the eel fighting—

my eyes have seen what my hand did.